Being Happy

Cheryl Caldwell

KPT PUBLISHING

Look for
the little things
in life.

I don't care how old I am, if I see a bubble, I will hunt it down and pop it.

The big things
will come.

If history repeats itself, I am totally getting a dinosaur.

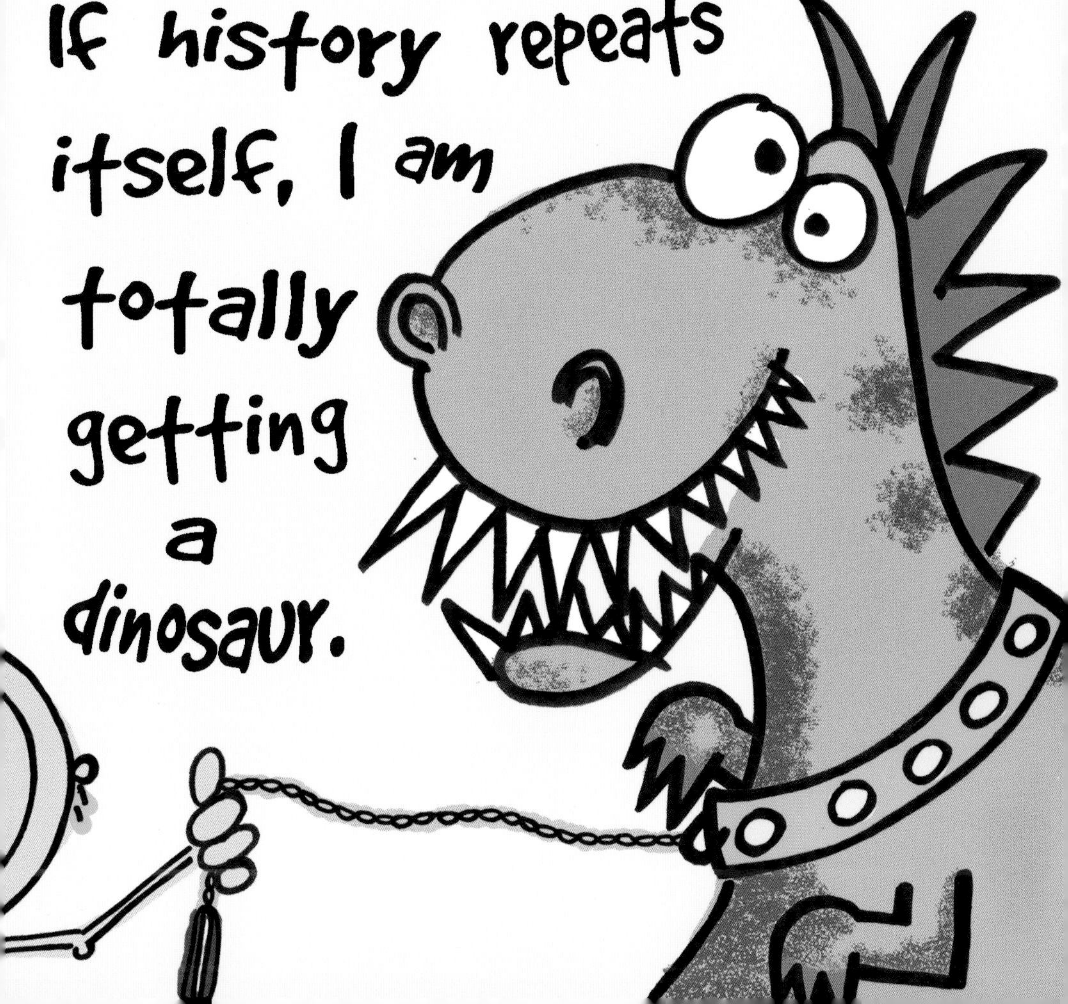

Leave the negative
stuff behind.

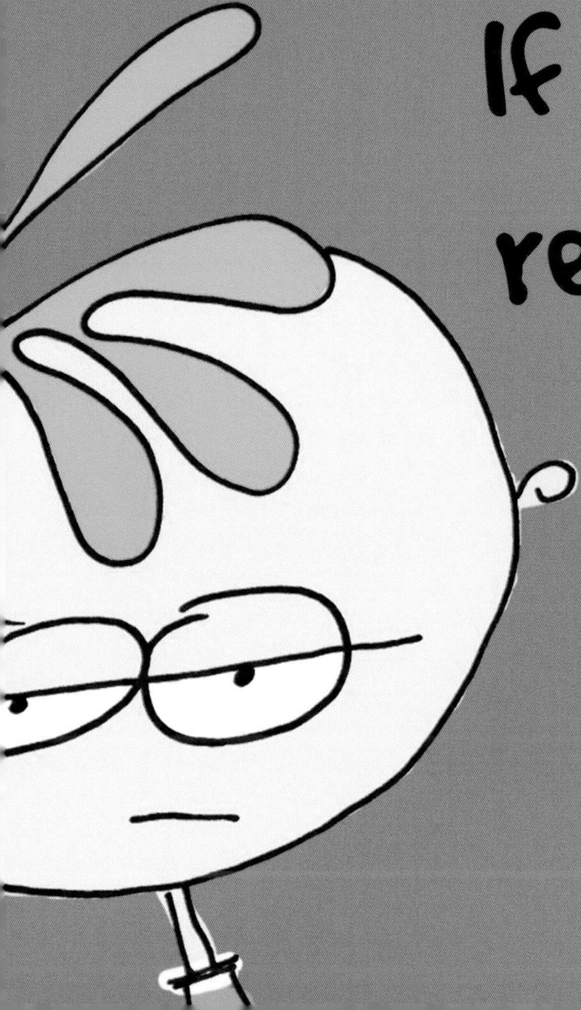

If I don't remember it, it didn't happen.

Take some
time for yourself.

I like to have a glass of wine to relax after a long glass of wine.

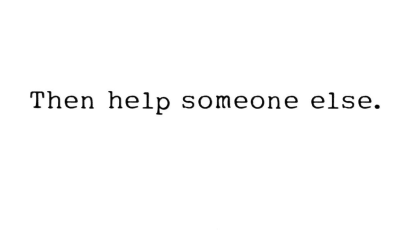

Then help someone else.

Give compliments.

I hate it when you give someone a sincere compliment on their mustache, and then suddenly she's not your friend anymore.

Surround yourself
with positive people.

If somebody says you use too much parmesan cheese, stop talking to them. You don't need that kind of negativity in your life.

Now you're ready
to take control.

I'm a leader–not a follower.

Unless it's dark–then I'm a follower.

You won't always
have the answers.

If life came with background music, I'd have a much better idea how to react right now.

But you're in front
more than you know.

And sometimes it's simpler than you think.

When
nothing
goes
right...

...go left.

You just have to change your perspective.

Try not to make things
more complicated
than they really are.

When I see a light flickering,
I think:
1% electrical problem,
99% demons.

Get out of
your own way.

You know you are really stressed when you start getting on your own nerves.

You are so much stronger
than you think.

Do something
that your future-self
will be happy about.

Stop making excuses.

In my defense,
I was left unsupervised.

Don't let fear
kill your dreams.

There is nothing to fear
but
fear itself...

and
spiders.

Definitely spiders.

Go ahead.
Dream Big.

If no one comes back from the future to stop you, how bad could the decision really be?

You won't be happy
when things change,
but things will change
when you are happy.

If you feel blue,....
start
breathing again.

It's a good day
to have a good day.

That sounds like an absolutely horrible idea.

What time?

You know all of the things
you've wanted to do?

You should
do them.

Because...

I don't mean to spoil the ending for you... But everything is going to be ok

About the Author

Cheryl **Caldwell** is a sometimes artist, photographer, filmmaker, marine aquarist, and author. Most of her inspiration comes from her unconventional view of the world and the fact that she finds the mundane hilarious. She is owner of Co-edikit®, a humor based company that pairs comical illustrations with a witty combination of clear cut, down-to-earth words of wisdom and sarcastic humor. Her artwork and characters have been licensed and sold throughout the world. Her original paintings of the Co-edikit® characters can be found in several art galleries in the U.S., including Bee Galleries in New Orleans. She still subscribes to the philosophy that if you're having a bad day, ask a four- or five-year-old to skip. It's hysterical.

Being Happy

Copyright © 2017 Cheryl Caldwell

Published by KPT Publishing
Minneapolis, Minnesota 55406
www.KPTPublishing.com

ISBN: 978-1-944833-09-1

Design and production by Koechel Peterson and Associates, Minneapolis, Minnesota

First printing March 2017

10 9 8 7 6 5 4 3 2 1

Printed in the United States of America